LET'S LOOK FOR NUMBERS

Bill Gillham *and* Susan Hulme

Photographs by
Jan Siegieda

Coward-McCann, Inc.
New York

one

one candle on Baby's cake

two

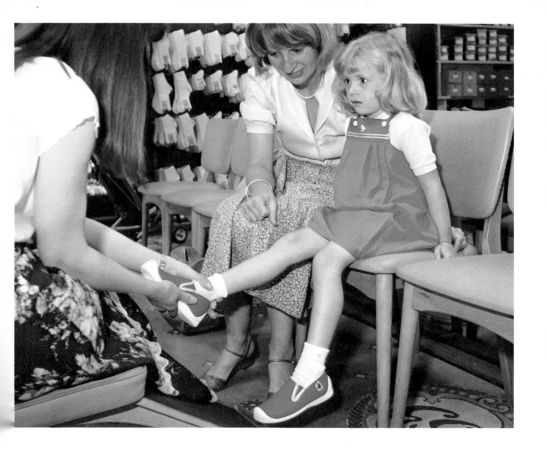

two new shoes for Jenny

three

three wheels on Daniel's tricycle

four

four slices of melon

five

five peas in a pod

six

six cherry cakes

seven

seven pegs for Baby to hammer

eight

eight cups make a tower

nine

nine bowling pins to knock down

ten

ten little toes

how many can *you* count?

LET'S LOOK FOR NUMBERS . . . is one of a series of four books designed to encourage children to *look* for the basic concepts of color, shape, number and opposites in their everyday world. By talking about the topics illustrated, children will be encouraged to think of other examples and so to develop further their mastery of language and thought, quite apart from the intrinsic pleasure of sharing books with a "helpful" adult.

Dr. Bill Gillham is a well-known educational psychologist and children's author, and senior lecturer in the Department of Psychology at the University of Strathclyde.

Susan Hulme is an experienced nursery school teacher, and mother of two young children, with a special interest in preschool education.

Jan Siegieda is a freelance photographer; these are his first children's books.

Text copyright © 1984 by Bill Gillham and Susan Hulme
Photographs copyright © 1984 Bill Gillham and Jan Siegieda
First American Edition 1984
All rights reserved. This book, or parts thereof, may not be
reproduced in any form without permission in writing from the publishers
First published by Methuen Children's Books, Ltd., London, England

Library of Congress Cataloging in Publication Data

Gillham, Bill.
  Let's look for numbers.

  Summary: Illustrates the numbers from one to ten,
using photographs and brief sentences or phrases.
  1. Counting – Juvenile literature. [1. Counting.
2. Number concept] I. Hulme, Susan. II. Siegieda,
Jan, ill. III. Title.
QA113.G55 1984   513′.2   83-24066
ISBN 0-698-20613-4

First printing
Printed in Great Britain